50 VEHICLES

Kids Coloring Book

NINALARS

This Book Belongs To

BUS

TAXI

HELICOPTER

UFO

MOTORCYCLE

SAILBOAT

EXCAVATOR

TRACTOR

PROPELLER PLANE

CONCRETE MIXER

FIRE TRUCK

TRAM

OFF ROAD TRUCK

RACE CAR

DUMP TRUCK

HOT AIR BALLON

TOW TRUCK

GARBAGE TRUCK

POLICE CAR

LOCOMOTIVE

COMBINE HARVESTER

AMBULANCE

SUBMARINE

BICYCLE

AIRPLANE

ROCKET

SHIP

CAR

CANOE

NARROWBOAT

ICEBREAKER

YACHT

QUAD BIKE

CRANE

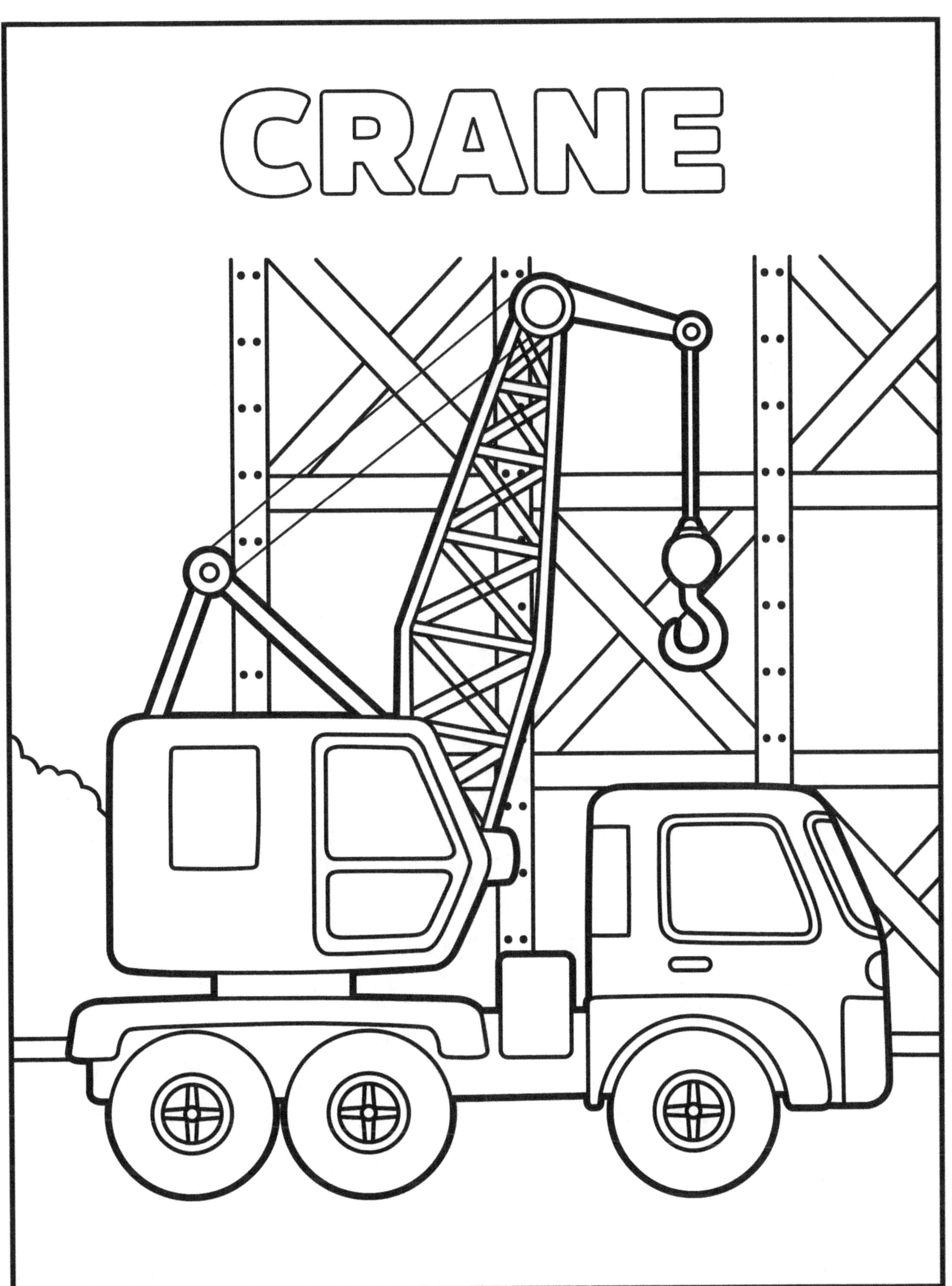

WAGON

JET SKI

COVERED WAGON

WATER TRUCK

NUCLEAR SUBMARINE

X-MAS SLEIGH

WINDSURFER

ICE CREAM TRUCK

KAYAK

JET FIGHTER

TRUCK

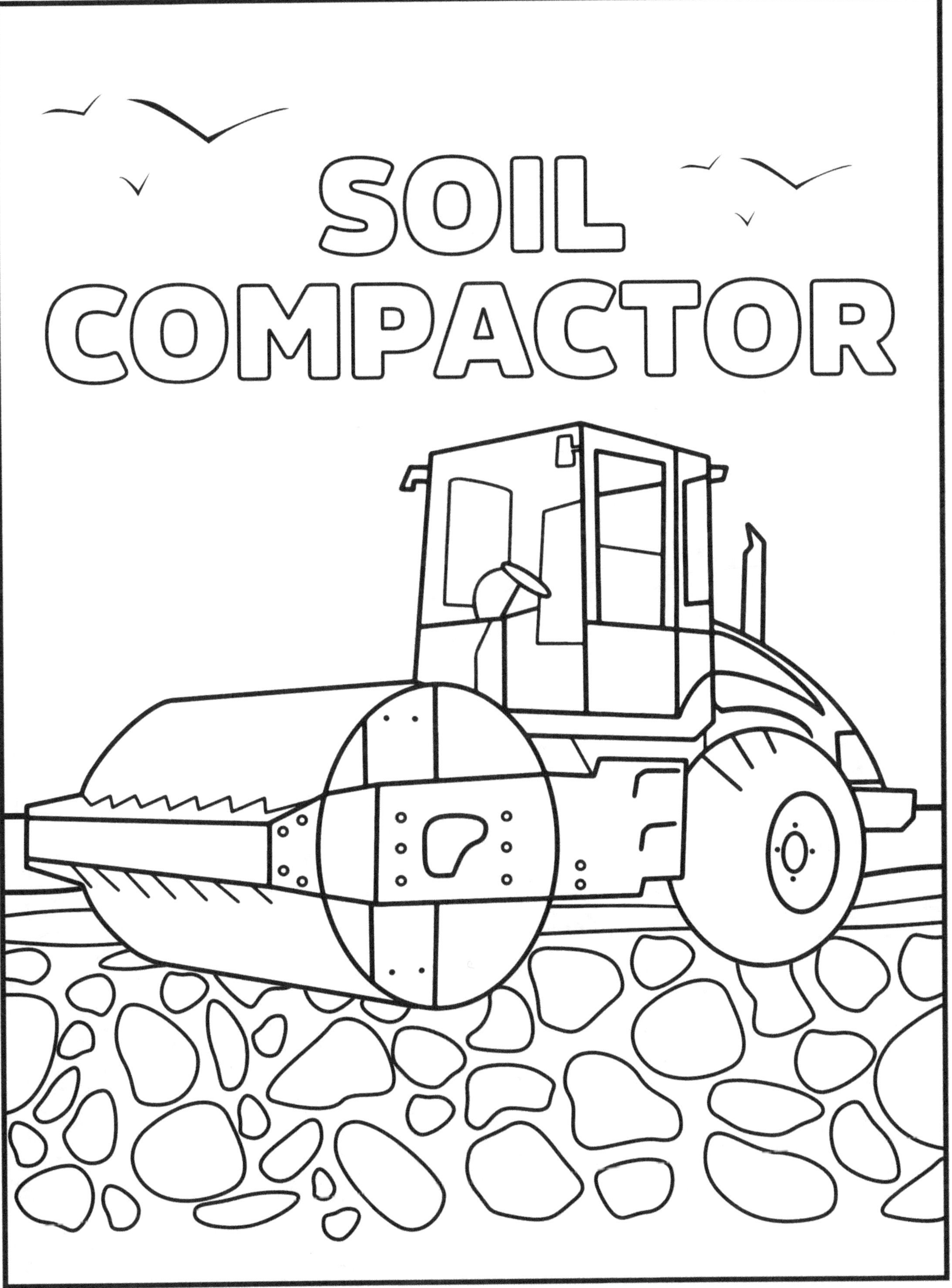

SOIL
COMPACTOR

FORKLIFT

ZEPPELIN

LIMOUSINE

SCOOTER